Patrick

✢

Saint of Ireland

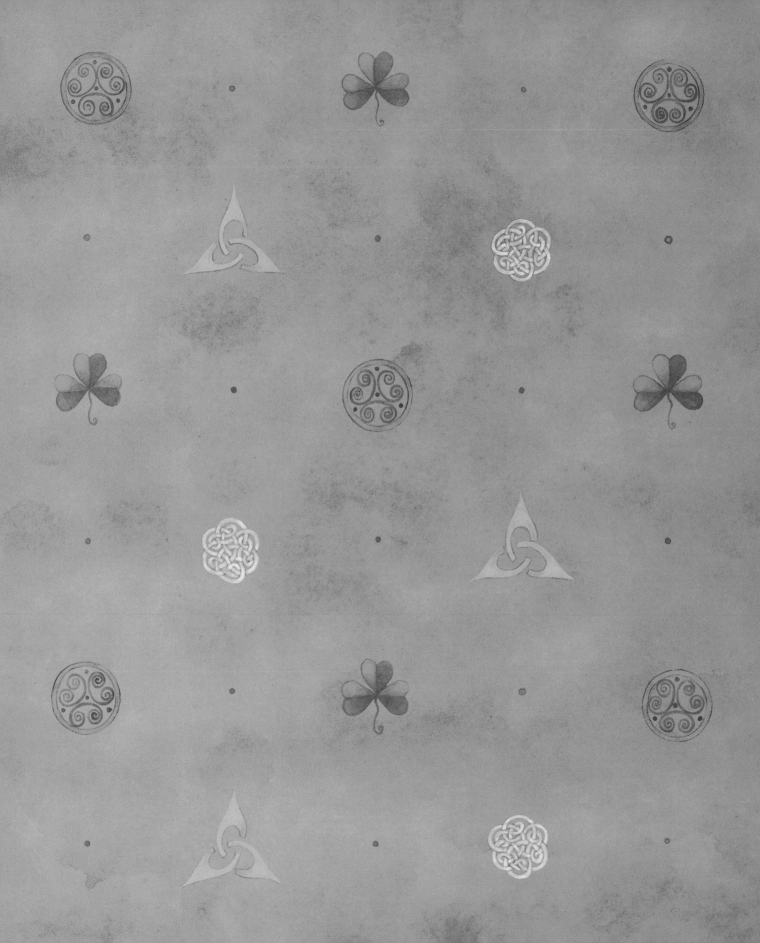

Patrick
†
Saint of Ireland

Joyce Denham

Illustrated by Diana Mayo

LION
Children's Books

For Uncle Jack
J.D.

For my model, Jake
D.M.

Published by
Lion Publishing plc
Mayfield House, 256 Banbury Road,
Oxford OX2 7DH, England
www.lion-publishing.co.uk
ISBN 0 7459 4565 1

First hardback edition 2002
First paperback edition 2002
1 3 5 7 9 10 8 6 4 2 0

Typeset in 16/24 Goudy Old Style BT
Printed and bound in China

Introduction

In the days when the great Roman Empire was crumbling and pirates began to invade the island of Britain, dreadful forces altered the destiny of a boy named Patrick.

No one suspected an attack.

No one felt any warning fears.

As on every other day, Patrick walked with his father, his mother and the other villagers to the church for evening prayers. Surrounded by the cool peacefulness of stone walls, they recited their faith.

'We believe in God Almighty,
Maker of all that exists,
And in God's Son, Jesus Christ,
And in the Holy Spirit…'

Patrick was barely interested in these words, and did not truly understand them. Like a stealthy fox, he slipped silently out of the door and ran into the dense woods. Every evening, he played the same game: he waited for the friendly deer to appear at the edge of a clearing. Then he bounded after them, running and leaping.

The dusk deepened and Patrick kept running. He didn't know that the Irish warlord Niall of the Nine Hostages and armies of his fierce pirates were rolling into the western forests of Britain like a huge black wave.

From out of nowhere vile sea robbers sprang at him, catching his long legs. 'Help!' Patrick shrieked. 'Let me go, you brutes! Help! Oh help!'

The deer, watching from behind the trees, were the only friends who heard his cries.

That night Niall and his men kidnapped thousands of Britons.
They flung them into stinking boats and then sailed far over the
water to Ireland, where they sold their prisoners as slaves.

Such misery and loneliness Patrick had never known. A man named Miliucc bought him at the slave sale and led him to a vast, bleak hillside overlooking the rough sea. Patrick tended Miliucc's sheep, living all alone with little food and no company.

In time, shepherds from the neighbouring hills befriended him
and taught him their Irish words. They were brave and rugged
herders, but at night, when the light failed and the shadows on the
edge of the forest lengthened, and the winds whined on the bare
hills, they feared that evil gods might swirl down among them.

Patrick, too, was afraid.

It was then that he remembered what his parents had taught
him – that God loved him and was always near. Now, as a homesick
slave, far, far away from the sound of his parents' voices, he heard
their words again in his heart, and at last he understood them.

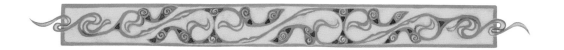

He prayed to God a hundred times each day and a hundred times each night. With God as his constant companion, Patrick's loneliness disappeared, and a love for Ireland slowly grew inside him. God opened his eyes to the beauties of his new country, the brilliance of its emerald hills, the ruggedness of its ancient stones. Now, morning after morning as the bright sun rose, Patrick raised his hands to heaven and sang this joyful song:

All things below, around, above,
Are held by hands of perfect love.
As heavenly Father, God is One,
Revealed on earth as God the Son –
Who was a man, and conquered death,
And with the Father gives me breath.
God's tender Spirit floods my soul,
Who calls me 'child', who makes me whole.
Creative Spirit-Father-Son
Is One in Three and Three in One!

Six long years went by. Then one night in a mysterious dream a voice spoke to Patrick saying, 'Now you will return to your own country. Behold, your ship is waiting!'

He woke as if to a thunderclap. All about him the blackness of night still lingered; but he felt as if a lightning bolt had lit up his whole world, and with the swiftness of a deer he ran from his hillside and his master. For days and days he ran.

God guided him to the eastern coast of Ireland. There, just as the voice had said, was a ship. The captain took him on board and they sailed back across the Irish Sea to Britain – to home.

When his parents laid eyes on their son, they could hardly believe it was Patrick. 'We thought you were dead!' they sobbed. Then they threw their arms around him and begged him to never leave them again.

Not many nights after, however, Patrick had another dream. A man named Victoricus came from Ireland, knocked on his door and handed him a letter on which were written these words: *The Voice of the Irish.*

Suddenly he heard it – a cry, made by the voices of the Irish people living near his old barren hillside. 'O holy boy!' they shouted. 'We beg you, come and walk among us once again!' Their pleading broke his heart, and when he woke, he knew that God had spoken to him.

So Patrick studied hard for many years, and when the time was right, he was made a bishop in the Christian church. Then he kissed his parents for the last time in his life and sailed for the land of his captivity.

Boldly he travelled from settlement to settlement, telling all those he met that God loved them and was always near. 'The God I worship is three in one,' he would tell them. Then he would stoop to the ground and pick a lovely green shamrock. 'You see?' he would ask. 'This beautiful leaf has three parts, yet it is one leaf. Even so, the true God has three faces, yet is one God: God the Father, God the Son (who is called Jesus), and God the Holy Spirit.'

Many believed Patrick's words and wanted to be close to the God who loved them. In the tradition of the church, he baptized them as a sign of their faith. Soon his new family was too large to count.

Many of the Irish chieftains, though, were suspicious of Patrick. Especially King Laoghaire*.

It was spring, the time of the pagan fire festival, and Laoghaire prepared a great feast at his palace on the hill of Tara. At the same time Patrick pitched his tents on the great plain near the king's estate. He, too, had something to celebrate: it was Easter – the festival of Christ's resurrection.

That night the earth lay shrouded in darkness, waiting for the first gleam of the newly-lit fire at Tara. For on the eve of the festival, if anyone kindled his fire before the king kindled his, that person must die.

* Pronounced 'Leary'

Patrick was unafraid. He and his followers defied the king and his pagan gods, and they lit an Easter fire that blazed with life.

Their hymns of praise to God rang through the valley; and
Laoghaire, and all the people of the plain who sat in darkness, saw
the great light.

In a rage the king and his warriors marched across the plain to kill Patrick. Still the Easter fire burned, and as Laoghaire approached, Patrick cried to God for protection:

The Deer's Cry
(A prayer of St Patrick)

In strength of sky and depth of sea,
I place my faith in God the Three.
With three-fold might protecting me
I rise in strength of Trinity.
Christ on my right
Christ on my left
Christ in the heights
Christ in the depths.
Behind, before,
Within, without,
Christ's power to compass me about.
Christ's ear to hear
Christ's eye to see
Christ's mind in all who think of me.

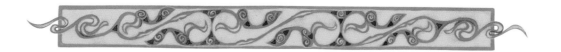

Suddenly, the war party halted. Where Patrick and his companions had stood, the king now saw only deer running into the forest. Fear gripped the hearts of Laoghaire and his men: the God of Patrick was surely greater than the gods of the fire festival.

After seeing the miracle of the Easter fire, so many people believed in God that Patrick decided to establish a church on the hill at Armagh. Some say that when all was ready to begin the building of the altar, a young fawn lay on the spot and would not move.

When the workers decided to kill her, Patrick cried, 'No! Do not touch her. She is a living stone in God's great cathedral of creation. Would you destroy a part of the cathedral to build one small church?' Then he tenderly carried the fawn on his shoulders and released her in the forest.

In time the church was completed, and Patrick led all its members in praise of their Creator.

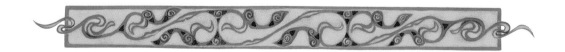

Thousands of Christians still worship in the churches that Patrick established. His love for the Irish people inspired them to honour him as their patron saint; and even today visitors walking in the woods near Armagh sense his spirit – like that of a wild deer, running and panting after God.

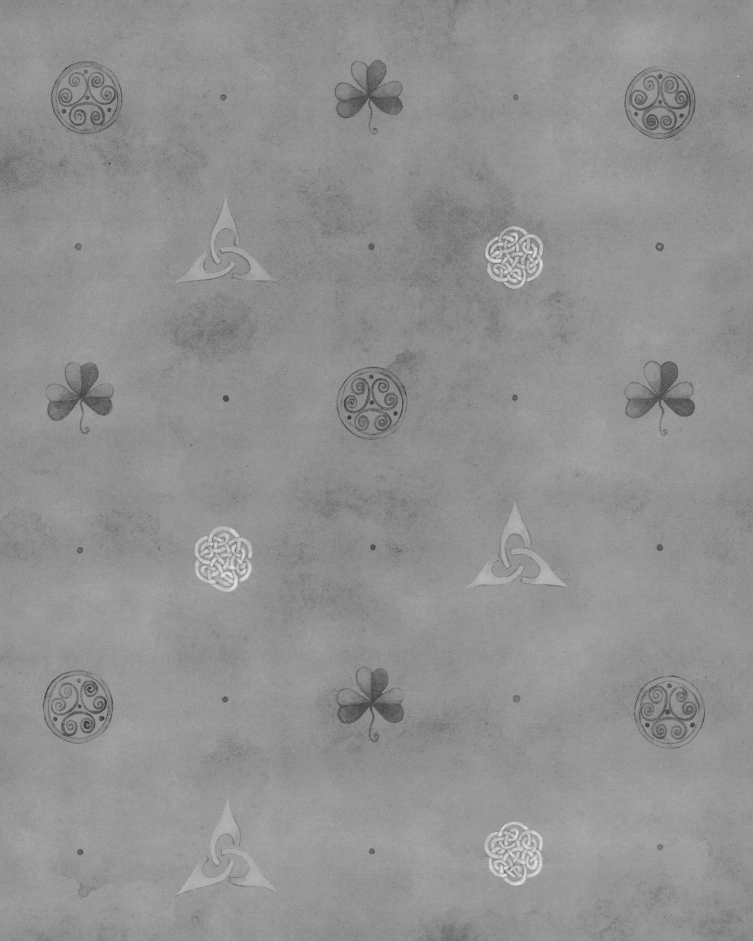

Also by Joyce Denham from Lion Children's Books

A Child's Book of Celtic Prayers

The Hard to Swallow Tale of Jonah and the Whale

Stories of the Saints

✢